MACMILLAN
BEGINNER

CW00507705

CHARLES DICKENS

A Tale of Two Cities

Retold by Stephen Colbourn

MACMILLAN

BEGINNER LEVEL

Founding Editor: John Milne

The Macmillan Readers provide a choice of enjoyable reading materials for learners of English. The series is published at six levels – Starter, Beginner, Elementary, Pre-intermediate, Intermediate and Upper.

Level control

Information, structure and vocabulary are controlled to suit the students' ability at each level.

The number of words at each level:

Starter	about 300 basic words
Beginner	about 600 basic words
Elementary	about 1100 basic words
Pre-intermediate	about 1400 basic words
Intermediate	about 1600 basic words
Upper	about 2200 basic words

Vocabulary

Some difficult words and phrases in this book are important for understanding the story. Some of these words are explained in the story and some are shown in the pictures. From Pre-intermediate level upwards, words are marked with a number like this: ...³. These words are explained in the Glossary at the end of the book.

Contents

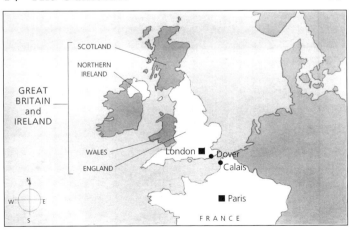

A Note About the Author

Charles Dickens was born on 7th February 1812. The Dickens family lived near Portsmouth, on the south coast of England. Later, the family lived in London.

Dickens had three brothers and three sisters. He was a small, thin boy. And he was often ill.

Dickens' father, John, was a clerk in an office. He worked for the British Navy. But John did not spend his money carefully. He owed people money. In 1824, he was sent to prison. Dickens' father, mother, brothers and sisters all stayed in the prison. Dickens had to work in a factory. He never forgot this difficult time.

Dickens went to school for only a few years. But he read many books and he educated himself. In 1834, Dickens became a newspaper reporter. He also wrote stories. His first stories were printed in magazines. A new part of the story was printed each week. These stories were very, very popular. Dickens became the most famous English writer in the nineteenth century.

Dickens loved London. He often walked through the streets. And Dickens visited the theatres, museums and gardens. Many of his stories are about life in London. Dickens wrote about the poor people, the hungry children and the bad houses they all lived in.

Dickens married Catherine Hogarth in 1836. They had ten children. But Catherine and Charles were not happy. In 1857 Dickens met an actress, Ellen Ternan. He fell in love with her. Dickens separated from his wife in 1858.

Dickens worked hard all his life. He became very rich. In 1856, he bought a large house – Gad's Hill – in Kent. He travelled in England, Scotland, Ireland and America. He read his stories in theatres.

Some of Dickens' stories are: *Oliver Twist* (1837–1839), *Bleak House* (1852–1853), *A Tale of Two Cities* (1859), *Great Expectations* (1860–1861), *A Christmas Carol* (1843), *Our Mutual Friend* (1864–1865).

Dickens died on 8th June 1870. He was 58 years old. He was buried in the famous church, Westminster Abbey, in London.

A Note About This Story

Time: 1775 to 1792. **Places**: London, England and Paris, France.

This was a time of wars and revolutions. Before 1789, there were kings in France. The last King of France was Louis XVI.

Rich and powerful people – aristocrats – governed France for King Louis. The aristocrats owned the land. They lived in large, beautiful houses – châteaux. Many poor people wanted to change the government. The people had little food and no money. These people wanted a revolution.

In 1776, there was a revolution in North America. The American Colonies wanted to be independent from England. They fought a war. The English were defeated. The American colonists called their country, the United States of America. Then the country was a Republic. It had a president, not a king. The first President of the USA was George Washington.

There was a revolution in France in 1789. The people sent King Louis to prison. There was a new revolutionary government. Many aristocrats escaped to other countries. But many were killed. King Louis XVI was killed. He was executed by guillotine.

At this time, people travelled in coaches. Coaches were pulled by horses. The roads were very bad. There were no trains or cars. Journeys were long and difficult. Men on horses took messages and letters. There were no post offices or telephones.

a guillotine

a coach

Note: St = Saint (e.g. St Antoine).

The People in This Story

Mr Jarvis Lorry
mɪstə 'dʒɑːvɪs 'lɒrɪ

Jerry Cruncher
dʒerɪ 'krʌntʃə

Miss Lucie Manette
mɪs luːsiː mæ'net

Miss Pross
mɪs 'prɒs

Doctor Alexandre Manette
dɒktɜː ælek'sɑːndr mæ'net

Monsieur Ernest Defarge
mə'sɪjə 'eərnest də'fɑːrʒ

Madame Thérèse Defarge
mæ'dæm tɪ'reəz də'fɑːrʒ

Mr Charles Darnay
mɪstə tʃɑːlz 'dɑːneɪ

Mr Stryver
mɪstə 'straɪvə

Mr Sydney Carton
mɪstə 'sɪdnɪ 'kɑːtən

John Barsad
dʒɒn 'bɑːsæd

The Marquis St Evrémonde
ðə mɑːˈkiː sænt 'eɪ vreɪməɔːnd

Théophile Gabelle
'teɪɒfiːl 'gæbel

1

To Dover

It was the year 1775. A coach was going from London to Dover. The road was wet and muddy. The horses pulled the heavy coach slowly.

A man on a horse came along the road behind the coach. He was riding quickly.

'Stop!' shouted the rider.

'What do you want?' asked the coach driver.

'I have a message!' shouted the rider. He stopped his horse in front of the coach. The coach also stopped.

'The message is for Mr Jarvis Lorry,' said the rider.

A man looked out of the window of the coach. He was about sixty years old and he wore old-fashioned clothes. He saw the rider and asked, 'What news do you bring, Jerry?'

'Do you know this man, sir?' asked the coach driver. 'There are robbers on this road.'

'I know him,' replied the old man. 'His name is Jerry Cruncher. He has come from my bank. Jerry Cruncher is a messenger, not a robber.'

'Here is a letter for you, Mr Lorry,' the messenger said. 'Mr Tellson wants you to wait at the Royal George Inn at Dover. A young lady will travel to Paris with you.'

'Thank you, Jerry,' Mr Lorry said. He took the letter. 'I will wait in Dover. Good night.'

18th November 1775

To Mr Jarvis Lorry

We have news from Tellson's Bank in Paris. Doctor Manette is alive. He is living at the wine shop of Monsieur and Madame Defarge in St Antoine, Paris. Doctor Manette is ill. He was in prison for eighteen years.

Lucie Manette - Doctor Manette's daughter - will meet you in Dover. Go to the Royal George Inn, in Dover. Wait for Lucie Manette there.

Lucie has never met her father. Take Lucie to Paris with you. Then bring Doctor Manette and Lucie back to London.

Tellson

Mr Lorry waited at the Royal George Inn at Dover. Miss Lucie Manette arrived the next day. She was about eighteen years old and she had long golden hair.

'Miss Manette,' said Mr Lorry, 'I work for Tellson's Bank. There is a Tellson's Bank in London and a Tellson's Bank in Paris. I often travel between the two cities.'

'Twenty years ago, your father came to Tellson's Bank in Paris,' said Mr Lorry. 'He left some money in the bank.'

'Yes,' said Lucie Manette. 'My father went to prison and he died. My mother told me about Tellson's Bank. My mother brought me to England. I was very young. I have lived in England all my life. But my mother taught me French.'

'My mother died a few years ago,' Lucie said. 'And Tellson's Bank took care of me.'

'Your father went to prison,' Mr Lorry said. 'But he did not go to court. There was no trial.'

'That is right,' said Lucie. 'My father died in prison.'

'No, my dear,' said Mr Lorry. 'I have news of your father. He did not die in prison. He is alive and he is living in Paris. I will take you to him.'

Lucie Manette put her hand to her face. 'Miss Pross!' she said loudly. Then she fainted. She fell into Mr Lorry's arms.

A large woman with red hair ran into the room.

'I will take care of her!' she shouted. 'I am Miss Pross – Miss Manette's companion.'

2

A Wine Shop in Paris

Mr Lorry, Lucie Manette and Miss Pross went by ship from Dover to Calais. Then they went by coach to Paris. They found the Defarges' wine shop in St Antoine.

A wooden barrel of wine had broken in the street outside the wine shop. People were lying on the ground. They were drinking the wine. Their hands and faces were red. Monsieur Defarge, the owner of the wine shop, was standing outside the shop. He was watching the people in the street.

'Monsieur Defarge,' Mr Lorry said. 'My name is Jarvis Lorry. This is Miss Manette. Where is Doctor Manette? We are going to take him to England.'

'He is ill,' said Monsieur Defarge. 'My wife is taking care of him. Many years ago, I was Doctor Manette's servant. He helped us then. But he went to prison. Now we are helping him. Come in. Come and see him.'

Mr Lorry, Lucie, Miss Pross and Monsieur Defarge went into the wine shop. Madame Defarge was sitting in the shop. She was knitting with wool. Her face was hard and unkind.

'This is Mr Lorry,' said Monsieur Defarge. 'He wants to see Doctor Manette.'

'Doctor Manette will not know you,' said Madame Defarge. 'He was in prison for eighteen years. He remembers nothing.'

Madame Defarge looked at Lucie. 'Are you his daughter?' she asked.

'Yes,' said Lucie. 'I am Lucie Manette. I want to see my father.'

'Come with me,' said Madame Defarge.

Madame Defarge took Mr Lorry and Lucie upstairs to a small room. An old man was sitting in the room. His hair was white. He was making shoes.

Mr Lorry spoke to the old man. 'What is your name, Monsieur?' he asked.

The old man looked round. 'Prisoner Number One Hundred and Five, North Tower,' he replied.

'He knows his number in the Bastille Prison,' said Madame Defarge. 'But he does not know his name.'

Mr Lorry was a kind man. 'Come with us, Doctor Manette,' he said quietly. 'Your daughter is here. We will take you to England.'

Doctor Manette did not understand. Mr Lorry held the old man's arm. He led him out of the room. Doctor Manette walked slowly. He held a pair of shoes in his hand.

———

Mr Lorry took Doctor Manette, Miss Pross and Lucie back to England. They went by ship from Calais to Dover.

On the ship, Doctor Manette was weak and ill. A young man helped Lucie and Mr Lorry. They took care of Doctor Manette.

'You are kind, sir,' Lucie said to the young man. 'What is your name?'

'My name is Charles Darnay,' replied the young man.

'Are you French?' asked Lucie.

'Yes, I am,' Charles Darnay replied. 'But I live in England. I often travel between England and France.'

'My father has been ill for a long time,' said Lucie. 'But he will get well in England.'

'We will meet again,' said Darnay. 'I will visit you in England.'

———

In England, Doctor Manette slowly got well. After many months, he started to remember things. He remembered his wife. He remembered his daughter. But he did not remember the Bastille Prison. And he did not remember his journey to England.

Lucie and her father lived in a small house in London. Miss Pross lived with them. She took care of the house. Mr Lorry became a friend of the Manettes and Miss Pross. He often visited them.

One day, Doctor Manette and Lucie received a letter. It was a letter from a lawyer.

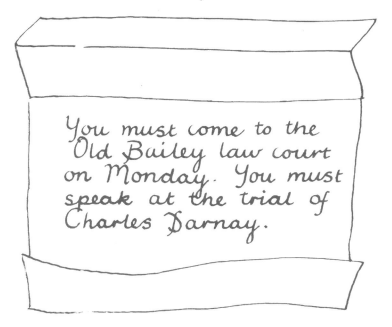

You must come to the Old Bailey law court on Monday. You must speak at the trial of Charles Darnay.

3

The Old Bailey

Charles Darnay stood in the courtroom. He stood in front of the judge and the jury. Doctor Manette, Lucie and Mr Lorry sat at the back of the courtroom.

A lawyer stood up.

19

The lawyer spoke to the judge and the jury.

'Charles Darnay travelled many times between England and France,' the lawyer said. 'There are some witnesses. These people saw Darnay in Dover and in Calais. One witness saw Darnay giving some papers to a Frenchman. Darnay is a spy.'

The first witness was Lucie Manette. Lucie went to the front of the courtroom. She answered the lawyer's questions.

'Did you see Charles Darnay on a ship?' the lawyer asked.

'Yes, I did,' Lucie replied. 'We were travelling from France to England. Mr Darnay often travels between England and France.'

'Did he speak about the American Colonies?' the lawyer asked.

'No, he did not.'

Then the lawyer asked Doctor Manette and Mr Lorry the same questions. Doctor Manette did not remember his journey from Paris to London. Mr Lorry had not spoken to Charles Darnay.

'Did you see Darnay on the ship?' the lawyer asked.

'Yes,' said Mr Lorry.

The next witness was a man with a crooked nose. His name was Barsad.

'Mr Barsad,' the lawyer began. 'Do you often travel to France?'

'Yes, sir, I do,' answered Barsad.

'Did you see Charles Darnay at Calais?'

'Yes, sir, I did. I saw him give some papers to a Frenchman.'

Another lawyer stood up. He was Charles Darnay's lawyer. His name was Stryver.

'Mr Barsad, what is your business in France?' Mr Stryver asked.

'It is private business, sir,' Barsad answered.

'Do you give letters or papers to Frenchmen some-times?' asked Mr Stryver.

'Yes, sir,' Barsad replied.

'Charles Darnay also has private business in France. Why are his papers different from yours?'

'Darnay gave papers to a spy,' said Barsad angrily. 'Darnay met the spy at night. I heard them speak about George Washington. Washington is a revolutionary in the American Colonies.'

'You saw Darnay and the French spy at night?' asked Mr Stryver. 'Did you see Charles Darnay clearly?'

'Yes, sir,' replied Barsad. 'I never forget a face.'

Mr Stryver's clerk was sitting next to him. Stryver pointed to this man. 'Mr Barsad, look at my clerk,' he said. 'Have you seen this man before?'

Everybody in the courtroom looked at Mr Stryver's

clerk. The clerk was exactly like Charles Darnay!

Mr Barsad did not answer Stryver's question.

'This is my clerk, Mr Sydney Carton,' said Mr Stryver. 'Is he like Charles Darnay?'

'Yes, he is,' Barsad replied.

'Did Mr Carton give some papers to a French spy in

Calais?' asked Stryver.

'No, sir.'

'It was dark,' said Stryver. 'You saw a man. The man was not Mr Carton. And he was not Charles Darnay.'

Everybody looked at Sydney Carton again. He was exactly like Charles Darnay. Mr Stryver was right.

The twelve men of the jury left the courtroom. They had to make a decision. Was Darnay Guilty? Or was he Not Guilty?

A few hours later, the jury came back into the courtroom.

The judge spoke to one of the jurymen. 'What is your decision?' he asked.

'Not Guilty,' said the juryman. 'Darnay is innocent. He is not a spy.'

4

New Friends

Charles Darnay was free. He stood outside the Old Bailey law courts. He shook hands with everybody.

Doctor Manette looked at Darnay. 'Do I know you?' Manette asked.

'He helped us on the ship, Father,' said Lucie. 'But you do not remember our journey to England.'

Charles Darnay and Sydney Carton went to an inn and drank some wine. Carton drank a lot of wine.

'You have drunk too much,' said Darnay. 'Do not drink any more, Mr Carton.'

'I always drink too much,' said Carton. 'I don't care about people. People don't care about me. But I want to drink some wine. And I want to think about Miss Lucie Manette. She is very beautiful.'

Charles Darnay and Sydney Carton looked at each

other. They were different in some ways. Darnay was tall and handsome. He had smooth, dark hair and he wore fine clothes. Carton had very pale skin and dark eyes. His hair and clothes were untidy. But the two men were like each other. Their faces were the same.

———

Four months later, Mr Jarvis Lorry went to Doctor Manette's house. The doctor and Lucie were not there. Mr Lorry talked to Miss Pross.

'How is Doctor Manette?' asked Mr Lorry.

'He is well,' replied Miss Pross. 'But sometimes he remembers the Bastille Prison. Sometimes he walks round and round his room. He remembers his work in the prison. He makes shoes.'

'Why did he go to prison?' asked Lorry. 'Has he told you?'

'No,' said Miss Pross. 'But a rich and powerful man sent him to the Bastille. In France, powerful aristocrats often send men to prison. Rich men make the laws. Innocent men go to prison, without a trial.'

'Yes,' said Lorry. 'French aristocrats send men to prison without a trial.'

'But, now, Doctor Manette's friends help him,' said Miss Pross. 'You are kind to him, Mr Lorry. And Mr Darnay and Mr Carton often visit our house.'

'I like this house,' said Mr Lorry. 'I do not have a family of my own. I visit this house and I am happy.'

5

The Aristocrat

It was a hot day in Paris. The Marquis St Evrémonde was angry. He left the palace of the King's Minister.

The Minister had not spoken to St Evrémonde. The Minister was too busy. He was drinking chocolate.

The Marquis got into his coach.

'Go quickly,' he shouted to the driver. 'Drive to the château!'

The coach went quickly through the streets of Paris. People ran away. People were afraid of the Marquis. They were afraid of the Marquis' coach and horses.

Suddenly, there was a terrible cry. The driver stopped the horses at the side of the road. People came out of their houses.

The Marquis shouted to the coach driver, 'What is wrong?'

'Monsieur the Marquis,' said the driver. 'A child ran in front of the coach. The horses kicked the child.'

'The child is dead!' shouted somebody in the crowd.

'Dead!' cried a tall man. 'Jacques, my child, is dead!'

'Who is the father of the child?' shouted the Marquis.

'It is Gaspard,' said a voice.

'Gaspard!' shouted the Marquis. 'Here is some money.'

The Marquis threw a gold coin out of the window of the coach. Nobody moved. Nobody picked up the coin. Everybody was afraid of the Marquis. They were afraid of rich and powerful aristocrats.

Then, somebody threw the gold coin back into the coach.

The aristocrat looked at the crowd of people. He hated them. He spoke to the coach driver.

'Drive to the château,' he said.

The coach moved away from the crowd. The Marquis forgot about the dead child. A man ran after the coach. But the Marquis did not see him.

———

In the evening, the coach arrived at the Château of St Evrémonde. Gabelle, an old servant, was waiting for the Marquis.

'Monsieur the Marquis,' said Gabelle. 'I was watching your coach. A man was holding on to the back of the coach.'

'A man? Where is he?' asked the Marquis.

'He jumped into the bushes beside the road,' replied Gabelle.

'Find him, quickly!' shouted the aristocrat. 'Now, has Monsieur Charles arrived? Has he come from England?'

'No, Monsieur the Marquis,' Gabelle replied.

Later in the evening, the Marquis was in his dining-room. He was eating his supper. He looked out of the window. He saw a man outside.

'Gabelle!' shouted the Marquis loudly. 'There is a man outside the château. Who is he?'

Gabelle looked out of the window. The night was dark.

'There is nobody outside, Monsieur the Marquis,' the servant said.

Then Gabelle listened. 'But I can hear something,' he said. 'I can hear a coach.'

'Good! My nephew Charles has arrived,' said the Marquis.

A few minutes later, Charles Darnay came into the dining-room.

'Good evening, Uncle,' he said.

'Good evening, Charles,' said the Marquis. 'How is your life in England?'

'My life is good, Uncle,' replied Charles Darnay.

'Why do you live in England?' said the Marquis. 'You must come back to France. Soon I will die. Then, you will be the Marquis St Evrémonde.'

'I do not want to be a Marquis,' said Darnay. 'I do not use the name St Evrémonde. I do not want to be an aristocrat.'

'Nonsense!' said the Marquis angrily. 'You *are* an aristocrat. We shall talk about this tomorrow.'

'I do not want to talk about this, Uncle,' Darnay replied. 'I will return to England early in the morning. Good night.'

———

The Marquis went to bed. He remembered the dead child in Paris. He remembered the tall man. The man had cried out, 'Dead! My child is dead!' Gabelle had seen a man holding on to his coach. The Marquis remembered that. He, himself, had seen a man outside the window of the château. He remembered that. Suddenly, the Marquis was afraid.

Charles Darnay left the château early in the morning. He did not speak to his uncle. He did not want to speak to his uncle. And Charles could not speak to him.

The Marquis St Evrémonde was dead. He lay in his bed. A knife was in his chest.

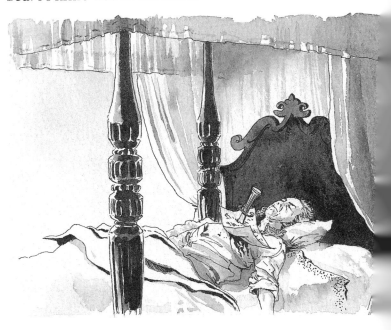

6

A Wedding

One day in the summer, Charles Darnay visited Doctor Manette at his house in London.

'Sir,' he said. 'I am a teacher and a translator. I am a Frenchman. But I live in England. Life in France is too difficult.'

'Yes, yes,' said Doctor Manette. 'There is only bad news from France.'

'I have often visited your house,' said Darnay. 'You are a kind man and a good doctor. And I am in love with your daughter. Sir, I want to marry Lucie.'

Doctor Manette was surprised. 'Does Lucie know this?' he asked.

'No,' replied Darnay. 'I will ask her today. Sir, will you let me marry Lucie?'

'Yes,' said Doctor Manette. 'Please speak to her.'

———

A few days later, Monsieur Defarge was in his wine shop in Paris. He had some news.

'Gaspard is dead,' Defarge said to his wife. 'He went to the guillotine. He died today.'

'Gaspard killed the Marquis St Evrémonde,' said Madame Defarge. 'But the people have suffered too much. The cruel aristocrats made the old laws. Now the people must make new laws. Soon we will kill all the aristocrats.'

'Be careful!' said Monsieur Defarge quickly. 'Those are dangerous words. There is a stranger in St Antoine. He speaks French well, but he is English. He is a spy. His name is Barsad.'

At that moment, Barsad himself came into the shop. 'Good afternoon,' he said. 'The news about Gaspard is bad.'

'He killed the Marquis St Evrémonde,' said Madame Defarge, carefully. 'And now he is dead.'

'Why did Gaspard kill the Marquis?' asked Barsad.

'Gaspard was a bad man. He was executed,' said Monsieur Defarge.

'Was the Marquis a bad man too? Was he executed too?' asked Barsad.

'We know nothing about that,' Monsieur Defarge said quickly.

Barsad bought a glass of wine. 'There is a new Marquis St Evrémonde,' he said.

'Yes. He is the nephew of the old Marquis,' replied Madame Defarge.

'The nephew – Charles. He lives in England,' Barsad said slowly. He looked at Madame Defarge.

'Does he live in England?' said Madame Defarge. She did not look at Barsad.

'I know about you,' said Barsad. 'Doctor Manette came out of the Bastille Prison. You took care of him. Is that true?'

'Everybody knows that,' said Madame Defarge. 'Many years ago, my husband was the doctor's servant. The doctor helped my family.'

'Why did Doctor Manette go to prison?' asked Barsad. 'Did St Evrémonde send him to the Bastille?'

'We do not know, Monsieur,' said Madame Defarge. 'You must not speak about this.'

'Very well,' said Barsad. 'But I can tell you some news. Doctor Manette's daughter – Lucie – is going to get married. She will be married in London. In England, her husband is called Charles Darnay. But in France he has another name. He is Charles, Monsieur the Marquis St Evrémonde.'

―――

One sunny day in London, Charles Darnay married Lucie Manette. Mr Jarvis Lorry and Mr Sydney Carton came to the wedding. It was a happy day.

But Sydney Carton was not very happy. He shook Charles Darnay's hand. He kissed Lucie.

'You are my good friends,' he said. 'I do not have many friends. Now you are married. Please let me visit your new house sometimes.'

'You will be welcome,' said Darnay. 'We will always be your friends.'

7

Revolution

Several years passed. Charles and Lucie Darnay had a daughter. They called the girl Lucie – like her mother.

Sydney Carton and Jarvis Lorry often visited the family.

One night, in July 1789, Mr Lorry visited the house.

'I have come from Tellson's Bank,' said Mr Lorry. 'There was a lot of work today. I have news from Paris. It is not good news.'

'The people are fighting in the streets of Paris,' said Mr Lorry. 'They have opened the Bastille Prison. All the prisoners are free.'

'There is a revolution in France,' Mr Lorry said. 'The people want a republic. They do not want a king. The people want a new government but they do not want the aristocrats.'

'There are many trials and many executions in Paris,' the banker said.

'The people watch the executions. The guillotine cuts off many heads. It cuts off the heads of the aristocrats.'

'Each time an aristocrat dies,' said Mr Lorry. 'The people are happy. "Death to all aristocrats!" they shout. "Long live the Republic! Long live the Revolution!"'

Outside the Château of St Evrémonde, the people were very angry.

'Kill all the aristocrats! Burn the château!' they shouted.

The servant, Gabelle, wanted to save the château. But nobody helped him. The people lit fires. The château burnt to the ground.

The people wanted to kill the Marquis St Evrémonde. But they could not find the Marquis. The old Marquis was dead. The new Marquis never came to France.

The people sent Gabelle to prison. 'Where is the Marquis?' they asked him. 'Only the Marquis can save you.'

In the next months, many French aristocrats came to London. They brought news from Paris.

Charles Darnay was now the Marquis St Evrémonde. But he did not tell anybody. It was a secret.

One day, Charles received a letter from France.

Prison of the Abbaye

Paris

To Monsieur Charles, the Marquis St Evrémonde —.

Please help me. I am in prison. I was the servant of your family. Soon I will die. Please come to Paris. Please help me.

Your family servant —

Théophile Gabelle

8

To Paris

Charles Darnay spoke to Mr Lorry.

'I must go to Paris,' he said. 'I must help a servant of my family.'

'Paris?' said Mr Lorry. 'Doctor Manette will be very worried. Your family will be very worried.'

'Please do not tell my family today,' said Darnay. 'Tell them tomorrow. Tomorrow, I will be in Paris. And soon, I will be back in London.'

'Very well,' said Mr Lorry. 'I, too, must go to Paris soon. I must get some papers from Tellson's Bank in Paris. I must bring them back to London. Paris is very dangerous now. The Revolution has made people wild.'

'Then I will send a message to you at Tellson's Bank,' said Darnay. 'I will meet you in Paris.'

_____

Charles Darnay went by ship from Dover to Calais. Many things in France had changed. There were many revolutionary guards in every town.

French people no longer called each other 'Monsieur' or 'Madame'. Everybody had to be called 'Citizen' or 'Citizeness'. Everybody was equal in the new Republic. There were no aristocrats. There was no king.

Charles went from Calais by coach. Outside the town, the coach stopped. Revolutionary guards were standing in the road.

'Who are you, Citizen?' one of the revolutionary guards asked.

'Show us your papers,' said another guard. 'Do you have a travel permit? What is your business in France?'

'I am going to Paris,' said Darnay. 'Please let me go on.'

'This man is an aristocrat,' said the first guard. 'He left France and he went to England. He must go to the guillotine.'

'I am going to Paris on business,' Darnay said.

'Yes, you are going to Paris,' said the second guard. 'You are going to prison. You are under arrest!'

'Why am I under arrest?' asked Darnay, angrily.

'You are an aristocrat,' said the first guard. 'All aristocrats are enemies of the Revolution and enemies of the Republic. All aristocrats are enemies of the people. The guillotine is waiting! It is waiting for you!'

A crowd of people stood around the coach. 'Death to all aristocrats!' they shouted. 'Take him to Paris!'

———

The revolutionary guards took Darnay to Paris. They put him in La Force Prison. They found the letter from Gabelle in his coat.

'This is a letter to St Evrémonde,' said a guard. 'We know that name. The people hate that name.'

The next day, a man visited Charles. The man was a revolutionary official. He looked at Darnay.

'I know your face,' he said. 'You are St Evrémonde. I am Citizen Defarge.'

'Monsieur Defarge,' said Darnay. 'I know your name. You helped Doctor Manette.'

'You must call me Citizen. We are all equal now. There are no more Monsieurs and Marquises.'

'Citizen Defarge, will you take a message to Tellson's Bank?' asked Darnay. 'It is a message for Mr

Lorry. He will give the message to Doctor Manette.'

'I will not take your message,' said Defarge. 'You are an aristocrat. You are an enemy of the Republic.'

'What will happen to me?' asked Darnay.

'There will be a trial in the People's Court. Then you will go to the guillotine,' said Defarge.

9

An Enemy of the Republic

Mr Lorry was at Tellson's Bank in Paris. He got some news. It was bad news. Charles Darnay was in La Force Prison.

Immediately, Mr Lorry sent a message to London. He sent it to Doctor Manette. Doctor Manette came to Paris with Lucie and her child. Miss Pross and Jerry Cruncher came too. They stayed in rooms near the bank.

Doctor Manette spoke to Mr Lorry.

'I was a prisoner in the Bastille Prison for eighteen years,' he said. 'The revolutionaries will listen to me. I will speak at Charles' trial. And I will speak to Monsieur and Madame Defarge. They will help us.'

'I will speak to Madame Defarge too,' said Lucie. 'I am a wife and I am a mother. Madame Defarge will understand. She will help us.'

Lucie went to the wine shop in St Antoine. She spoke to Madame Defarge. But Madame Defarge would not help her.

'Your husband is an aristocrat,' she said. 'Now he is in prison. Before the Revolution, the aristocrats sent poor people to prison. We were helpless.'

'Now all that is finished,' Madame Defarge said. 'The aristocrats are finished too. Your husband's trial will be tomorrow. I cannot help you.'

'Charles St Evrémonde, also called Charles Darnay!'

The President of the court shouted the name. Charles Darnay stood up. He stood in front of the judges. He answered their questions.

'You are an aristocrat and an enemy of the Republic,' said the President.

'No!' answered Darnay. 'I do not live in France. I have not treated the French people badly. I did not take money from the people. I do not want to be the Marquis St Evrémonde.'

'Are there witnesses?' asked the President. 'Will somebody speak for you?'

'Yes. Citizen Théophile Gabelle and Doctor Alexandre Manette will speak for me,' said Darnay.

Gabelle spoke first.

'Charles Darnay did not want to be the Marquis St Evrémonde,' he said. 'He did not want to be an aristocrat. He did not take any money from the people of France. He is a good man.'

Then Doctor Manette spoke.

'I was a prisoner in the Bastille for eighteen years,' he said.

The people in the courtroom cheered. 'Long live Doctor Manette!' they shouted.

'Charles Darnay helped me,' the doctor said. 'I was very sick and he took care of me. He married my daughter. He is a good man. He came back to France. He wants to help Citizen Gabelle.'

The people in the courtroom cheered again. 'Long live the Republic! Long live the people of France!' they shouted.

'Charles Darnay was arrested in England,' Doctor Manette said. 'The English said, "Darnay is a French spy. He is a friend of the revolutionaries in the American Colonies". Now, you say, "He is an enemy of France". You are wrong!'

'Let him go!' shouted the people in the courtroom. 'He is a friend of the Revolution!'

The judges made their decision.

'Not Guilty,' the President said. He spoke to Darnay. 'You are free!' he said.

10

Citizen Barsad

Charles Darnay stood outside the courtroom. He was free. He held Lucie in his arms.

'He is innocent. I have saved him,' said Doctor Manette. 'Let's go home now.'

They returned to their rooms near the bank. Jerry Cruncher and Miss Pross went out to buy some wine.

A little later, the doctor was talking to Charles and Lucie. Suddenly, some revolutionary guards came into the room.

'Why is he under arrest?' asked Doctor Manette. 'There was a trial. He is not guilty. He is free now.'

'There will be another trial tomorrow,' said the guard.

'What has he done wrong?' said Doctor Manette angrily. 'Who accuses him?'

'You will know tomorrow,' said the guard.

The guards took Darnay back to La Force Prison. Lucie cried. Her father held her in his arms.

'I have saved him once,' said Doctor Manette. 'I will save him again. I will speak at the trial tomorrow.'

———

Jerry Cruncher and Miss Pross were looking for some wine. They went into Monsieur and Madame Defarge's wine shop. Miss Pross saw a man inside the shop. She cried out, 'Solomon!'

'What do you want?' said the man, in English. He was angry.

'Solomon,' said Miss Pross. 'You are my brother, Solomon. I have not seen you for many years.'

'Be quiet!' said the man. 'I have a different name now. I am a revolutionary official. I am an important man in the Republic.'

'His name is Citizen Barsad,' said another man.

They all turned and looked at the person who had spoken.

'Darnay!' said Barsad. 'Why are you here?'

'No. I am not Charles Darnay,' said the man. 'My name is Sydney Carton. You saw me at the trial in

London. My face is like Darnay's face. But I am not Darnay.'

'I want to see Darnay and his wife, Lucie,' Carton said. 'Where are they?'

'Darnay is under arrest,' said Barsad. 'He is in La Force Prison. He will go to the guillotine!'

11

Doctor Manette's Letter

'You are Charles Evrémonde, also called Charles Darnay,' said the President of the Court. 'You are an enemy of the people.'

'Who accuses me?' said Darnay.

'Three citizens accuse you,' said the President. 'They are Ernest Defarge, Thérèse Defarge and Alexandre Manette.'

Doctor Manette stood up. 'I accuse no one,' he said.

'Sit down! Be quiet!' said the President. 'Citizen Defarge will speak.'

Defarge stood up. 'Citizens,' he said, 'I am a friend of the people. I fought well at the Bastille.'

The people in the courtroom cheered.

'I found a letter in the Bastille,' Defarge said. 'It was written by Doctor Alexandre Manette. He was Prisoner Number One Hundred and Five, North Tower.'

'Read the letter!' shouted the people in the courtroom.

Doctor Manette had written the letter many years before. He did not remember it.

Defarge read out the letter.

My name is Alexandre Manette. I am a doctor in Paris. I have a young wife. We are going to have a child.

One night, in December 1757, a coach came to my house. The man in the coach was an aristocrat.

'Please help me,' he said.

We went to a château outside Paris. A young woman lay in a bed. She was very sick. I looked at her.

'My husband, my father, my brother,' the young woman said. She said these words again and again. She had a fever. She was going to die.

There was a young man in another room in the château. He was badly injured.

'I am dying,' the young man said. 'They brought my sister to the château. They took away her husband. They killed our father. I am dying. Only my other sister, Thérèse, is free.'

'Who did this?' I asked.

'St Evrémonde,' the young man replied. Then he died. The young woman died a few hours later.

The aristocrat gave me some money. 'Take this money,' he said. 'Tell nobody about your visit here. You will be safe.'

A coach took me back to Paris. I was angry. I told my story to my wife and my servant. I told them the aristocrat's name – St Evrémonde. The next day, I was brought here to the Bastille. The Marquis St Evrémonde is a rich and powerful man. There was no trial. I am writing this letter in the North Tower of the Bastille Prison.

Defarge finished reading the letter.

'Doctor Manette was in prison for eighteen years,' he said. 'I, Ernest Defarge, was Doctor Manette's servant. My wife, Thérèse, was the dying girl's sister. Thérèse escaped from the aristocrats. Now we both say, "Death to St Evrémonde! Death to all aristocrats!" The prisoner must die!'

'Death to St Evrémonde!' shouted the people in the courtroom. 'Death to all aristocrats!'

'Charles St Evrémonde,' said the President of the Court. 'Your uncle was an enemy of the people. You are an enemy of the people. You must die. You will go to the guillotine tomorrow.'

The revolutionary guards took Darnay back to La Force Prison. Doctor Manette took Lucie to their rooms near the bank. Lucie cried and cried.

Sydney Carton was waiting in Doctor Manette's room. He spoke to Doctor Manette and Lucie.

'I have a plan,' he said. 'I will save Charles. You must travel early tomorrow. Mr Lorry will take you back to England. Do not wait in Paris. It is too dangerous. Charles will come to England with you.'

12

Sydney Carton's Plan

Sydney Carton went to Tellson's Bank and spoke to Mr Lorry.

'Please take Doctor Manette and Lucie to England tomorrow,' he said. 'They are in great danger. They are the family of an aristocrat.'

'Very well,' said Mr Lorry. 'I will go to London tomorrow. Will you come too?'

'Yes. I – or another man,' said Carton. 'The other man is like me.'

'What do you mean?' asked Lorry.

'I have a plan,' said Carton. 'I cannot tell you now. Here, take my travel permit. Someone will need it.'

He gave his papers to Lorry.

'I have always loved Lucie,' said Carton. 'I will do anything to help her. I want to save Charles.'

'But how? What will you do?' asked Lorry.

'John Barsad is a spy,' said Sydney Carton. 'Barsad is a revolutionary official. He is an important man in Paris. But he works for the English. He does not want the revolutionary guards to know that. He will help me. He must help me.'

'How will he help you?' said Lorry.

'He will take me into La Force Prison,' replied Carton. 'Mr Lorry, you must leave Paris tomorrow morning. You must leave with Doctor Manette and Lucie. Please, promise me this.'

'I promise,' said Mr Lorry.

Sydney Carton left Tellson's Bank. He went to a small shop in St Antoine. He bought a small bottle of liquid. It was a powerful drug.

Later, Mr Lorry spoke to Miss Pross.

'I will leave Paris early tomorrow,' he said. 'I will take Doctor Manette, Lucie and her child with me. They are in great danger. You must look after our things. You and Jerry will come to England the next day. You are English. The French people will not hurt you. You are not in danger.'

13

The Escape

In La Force Prison, Charles Darnay was writing a letter. He was writing to Lucie. Suddenly, the door opened. John Barsad and Sydney Carton entered. Darnay put down his pen.

'Sydney!' said Darnay. 'Why are you here?'

'I want to say goodbye, Charles,' Carton said.

'I am writing a letter to Lucie,' said Darnay. 'Will you take it to her?'

'Yes,' Carton replied.

Darnay looked down at the letter. He picked up his pen again. He started to write.

Carton took the bottle of liquid from his pocket. He put some of the liquid on his handkerchief.

He held the handkerchief against Darnay's nose and mouth.

The drug was very powerful. Soon, Darnay was asleep.

Quickly, Barsad!

Soon, Carton was dressed in Darnay's clothes. And Darnay was dressed in Carton's clothes. 'Now I am Charles,' Carton said. 'I will stay here, Barsad. Take Darnay away now!'

Barsad carried Darnay out of the room. He spoke to the guards.

'Mr Carton is ill,' he said. 'The English are not strong men. I must take him home.'

The guards laughed. Barsad carried Darnay away from the prison. A coach was waiting for them.

———

Early the next morning, some officials in a small town stopped a coach. The coach had come from Paris. It was travelling to Calais.

One of the officials spoke to the travellers.

'Show me your papers, Citizens,' he said. 'I must see your travel permits.'

Mr Lorry got out of the coach. He gave the official some travel permits.

'You are Lorry?' said the man. He looked at the other travellers. 'Alexandre Manette? Yes. Lucie Darnay and her child? Yes. And Sydney Carton?'

The official looked at the sleeping man. 'What is wrong with Carton?' he said. 'Is he ill?'

'Yes, he is ill. He is sleeping,' said Lorry.

'You will miss the executions on the guillotine today,' said the official. 'Fifty-two enemies of the Republic will be executed today. Are you going to Calais?'

'Yes,' said Lorry. 'Then to England, by ship.'

'Go on!' said the official.

The coach moved forward along the road. Lucie looked at the sleeping man – her husband, Charles.

'How did Charles escape from the prison?' asked Lucie.

'A very good friend has helped us,' said Mr Lorry. 'We will never be able to thank him.'

Soon, the coach was in Calais. A ship was waiting to take them to England.

14

The Guillotine

Miss Pross and Jerry Cruncher were in the rooms near the bank. They were putting Lucie Darnay's things into boxes. They were going to leave Paris later that day.

Suddenly, Madame Defarge came to Lucie's room.

'Where is the wife of St Evrémonde?' she shouted. 'She is an enemy of the people! She must not escape!'

Miss Pross stood in front of Madame Defarge. 'You cannot see her,' she said. 'You cannot come in.'

'I have something for her,' said Madame Defarge.

Madame Defarge lifted her arm. She was holding a pistol. She pointed the pistol at Miss Pross.

'Help me, Jerry!' Miss Pross shouted. 'This woman has a pistol!'

'Where is Lucie Darnay?' asked Madame Defarge.

Jerry ran to the two women. He held Madame Defarge's arm. He turned the pistol away from Miss Pross. There was a loud noise and a scream. Madame Defarge fell to the ground. She was dead!

'Come, Miss Pross!' said Jerry. 'We must leave Paris now.'

Soon, they were in a coach. They were travelling towards Calais.

———

Sydney Carton was travelling too. He had left La Force

Prison. He was sitting in a cart. There were many carts. Fifty-two people were going to the guillotine that morning.

There was a young girl in the cart with Carton.

'What have you done, my dear?' he asked her.

'I do not know,' the girl replied. She was crying. 'I am not an aristocrat. I am not a spy,' she said. 'But I am going to the guillotine.'

Carton held the girl's hand. 'You must be strong,' he said.

John Barsad was standing in the crowd. He watched the carts. They moved slowly towards the guillotine.

'Where is St Evrémonde?' asked a man.

Barsad pointed. 'He is there, in the first cart,' he said. 'He is holding the young girl's hand.'

'Death to St Evrémonde!' shouted the man.

'Death to St Evrémonde!' shouted the crowd.

'Be quiet!' said Barsad, quickly. 'Leave him in peace. He will die in five minutes.'

The crowd cheered.

The young girl spoke to Sydney Carton.

'Monsieur, are the people shouting your name?' she asked.

'Yes,' said Carton. 'I am St Evrémonde.'

'I am very frightened,' said the girl. 'Will you hold my hand until the end?'

'Yes,' said Carton. 'Look at me. Do not look at anything or anybody else.'

The cart stopped by the guillotine.

'You are a good man,' said the girl. 'Goodbye, Monsieur.'

'Goodbye, my dear,' said Carton. And he kissed her lips gently.

The revolutionary guards led the girl to the terrible guillotine. A moment later, the crowd cheered. The girl was dead.

Sydney Carton thought about his life. He was alone. He had no family. He had not been a good man. He had not always been kind to people. But he had known Lucie. He had loved her and he had cared for her family.

I am going to die. But Lucie and Charles are going to live. They will be happy. Now I am doing something good. Now at last, I can rest.

Carton walked towards the guillotine. The crowd cheered. 'Death to St Evrémonde!' they shouted. And Sydney Carton smiled.

Published by Macmillan Heinemann ELT
Between Towns Road, Oxford OX4 3PP
Macmillan Heinemann ELT is an imprint of
Macmillan Publishers Limited
Companies and representatives throughout the world
Heinemann is a registered trademark of Pearson Education, used under licenece.

ISBN 978 0 2300 3508 9
ISBN 978 1 4050 7606 7 (with CD pack)

This retold version by Stephen Colbourn for Macmillan Readers
First published 1997
Text © Stephen Colbourn 1997, 2005
Design and illustration © Macmillan Publishers Limited 1997, 2005

This edition first published 2005

Designed by Sue Vaudin
Illustrated by Gillian Hunt
Map on page 3 by John Gilkes
Typography by Adrian Hodgkins
Original cover template design by Jackie Hill
Cover illustration: 'Storming the Bastille' by Jean-Pierre Houel, 1789/Corbi

Printed in Thailand

2013   2012   2011
7   6   5   4

with CD pack

2013   2012   2011
11   10   9   8